"A MUST READ FOR WOMEN OF ALL AGES"

I WANT MY VAGINA BACK

by

Pamela Love Manning, PhD

Certified Professional Life Coach

D1444175

I WANT MY VAGINA BACK

Copyright @ 2010, PM Love Enterprises

All rights reserved. This book or parts thereof may not be reproduced in any form without permission from the author.

Printed in the United States of America: Createspace

ISBN-13: 978-1456329907
ISBN-10: 1456329901

Library of Congress *pending*

Cover Design by Kathy Patterson
Edited by: Nicole Goodman

To contact Dr. Pam: Love:

 PO Box 47133, Baltimore, Maryland 21244.
Email: lifedestination357@yahoo.com
URL: www.drpamlove.com

A Note to the Reader:
The information in this book is for entertainment purposes only. We strive to provide accurate, reliable, and complete information, but do not warrant that this is so. Stories are a blend of many true stories. All names have been changed.

This book is designed to provide information in regard to the subject matter covered. It is sold with the understanding that the author is not rendering professional advice. Readers are urged to seek the services of a competent professional, if applicable.

DEDICATION

I dedicate this book to every woman who chooses
to value her vagina!

FOREWORD

There is something special about the bond among the female human species. Regardless of our age or geographic locations, we just gravitate to each other. We talk to and about each other at the drop of a dime. From our homes, shoes, clothes, men and our children, we talk about any and everything. But unfortunately we don't authentically talk about the vagina. It's unfortunate, but perhaps our male counterparts have seen, touched, known, enjoyed and conversed more about this potent female genitalia than us. As women, we rarely talk openly and honestly about one of the most valuable parts of our bodies and sexual experiences that can have such a profound impact on our lives.

Billions of dollars are spent on vaginal diagnostic and surgical procedures performed each year ranging from pregnancy, childbirth, abortions, hysterectomies and pap smears. As mesmerizing as this organ is, our unfamiliarity, immaturity and ignorance about the vagina is often conveyed by common nicknames like cookie, kitty-cat, or poonanie, humorous terms that we frequently use and permit others to use to describe, define and devalue us.

Supposedly, we are trained to clean our vagina, keep it smelling fresh, and shave or wax the area surrounding it. Others are taught to intoxicatingly open and close it to control people and manipulate circumstances. Sisters live their lives spiritually, emotionally and psychologically detached from their vaginas.

Ironically though, we interact with our vaginas daily and allow others to interact with it or in some cases, there is a forced interaction. Either way, too often, we ignore the potential emotional, physical, social and financial costs associated with these interactions. Most importantly, we continue to ignore the value of our vaginas.

I applaud Dr. Love Manning for tackling this controversial yet, relevant topic. *I Want My Vagina Back* serves as a wakeup call for all females, young and old, and anyone that interacts with our vaginas that the days of neglect, ignorance, abuse, misuse and meaningless encounters are over! Regardless of our age or vaginal status (virginity, celibacy, sexually active, etc.) the days of not talking to one another about the impact sex has on our lives must cease. We can no longer sit by idle while millions of females are daily impacted by sexual abuse, vaginal displeasure, sexually transmitted diseases (STDs), infertility, vaginal infections, teen pregnancies, gynecologic cancers (cervical, ovarian, uterine, vaginal, and vulvar) and the emotional and financial costs associated with these undesirable outcomes.

I Want My Vagina Back is such a timely book because it propels us to a level of comfort, awareness and much needed sobriety to authentically dialogue about our vaginas without fear or ignorance. The more we learn, respect and cherish our vaginas, the more we can teach others to value our vaginas as well.

The book you have in your hands can change your life and the lives of women around you.

Sharon D. Jones-Eversley, DrPH
Relevant Solutions, CEO
Towson University, Assistant Professor

ACKNOWLEDGMENTS

I thank God for his love, grace, and faithfulness. Without Jesus Christ, I would be nothing. With Him, I will be all that He has destined me to be!

Since the release of my last book, many people have asked when I was going to write another book. Their encouragement along with Elder R. Kevin Matthews saying to me on July 19, 2010 "you need to write that book," resulted in my writing "I Want My Vagina Back." Thank you to everyone who wanted to read another one of my books. Special thanks to Elder R. Kevin Matthews of Evangel Cathedral for practicing what you teach, helping me to release my faith and guiding, mentoring, and supporting me in doing what God has called me to do.

Thanks to Bishop Don Meares of Evangel Cathedral for your vision, leadership, and a standard and spirit of excellence that has caused me to grow. Thanks to the elders, ministers, deacons, and friends at Evangel Cathedral.

Thanks to my husband, Maxwell Manning for his love, support, encouragement, and friendship. Thank you for always pushing me and unselfishly leading me in the direction of my purpose.

A big hug to my mom (Lenora Warren), sister, (Angela McCullum), brother (Wayne McCullum), and Mr. Johnny for their unwavering love and support. Hugs to my nieces and nephews, and my sisters and brothers-in-law (Belinda & David; Joan & Earle; Sara). . Another big hug to my biological children, grandson, godchildren, and "fictive" children: Glenn, Tiffany, Nicole, Corey, Jordan Joshua, Ricki, Jennifer, India, Tamika, Martena, Martin, and the ladies of "Sisters of Nia."

Thanks to CJ for our conversation during the summer of 2010. You spoke to the "me" few people know and confirmed that God was calling me to share my gifts. Thanks to Stephanie, Kim, Deanna, my daughter Nicole, and Nicole G. for previewing the book and giving me constructive feedback.

A big hug to members of the Warren, Myles, Bowie, Manning, Davis, Pulley, Johnson, Thomas, McCullum, McCullough, and Duncan families as well as Amina, April, Benita, Camilla, Cara, Christina & Phil, CJ & Rick, David, Darlene & Federico, Debbie, Delois, Denise & Larry, Denise W., Dorenzer & Phillip, Dr. Harvey, Dr. Born, Dr. Diggs, Dr. Raheim, Dr. Janice Stevenson, Ena, Esther & Bernard, Joyce D., Kim & Latif, Larry J, Linda & Marvin, Lucia, Lynn, Martina, Mike & Terrie, Ms. Edith, Mrs. Gold, Pam, Randy, Ron T., Sabrina, Sharon, Tina & Mark, Apostle and Bishop Montgomery, Bishop & Nisey Elliott, Pastor Draper, and Pastor Bethea.

Thanks to: Dr. Polston, my colleagues and many of the students in the Dept. of Social Work, College of Professional Studies at BSU; members of my Coppin State University family (including Dr. and Mrs. Avery), members of the CSU Development Foundation Board, staff and members of USM's Development Foundation, faculty & staff at UMB School of Social Work, Roy Cox Photography, my "blue and white" family, and the wonderful ladies at the PAL Day Salon.

Final thanks to Kathy for the perfect book cover and your assistance in getting this book to the printer; to Ebony for assistance with prelaunch activities and PR; Tim for the audio version of this book and Marla for the conversation that led to the idea for this book.

INTRODUCTION

Several years ago, I had a conversation with a friend that sparked the idea for this book. My friend was having some challenges with her ex-husband and father of her sons. Our conversation led to us reminiscing about past relationships and personal regrets. We laughed about each other's relationships and some of the poor choices we had made. We also expressed some confusion as to why we chose to have sex with certain men. All of a sudden, without hesitation and with a fluctuation in her tone, my friend said "You know, there are times I just want to knock on the doors of some of the men I slept with and say I WANT MY VAGINA BACK!" As if this was humanly possible, I proclaimed, "Me too!" Although we laughed, we realized this was no laughing matter. It donned on us that we regretted letting men open us up and dump inside of us as if we were a trash can. We understood and had discussed many of the ways that those sexual encounters caused us to suffer emotionally, physically, and socially.

I think my friend and I hung up the phone wishing we could erase the times we had sex from the fabric of our lives, but knew that we were stuck with the memories and the consequences of our behavior.

That conversation stayed with me for a long time. Its message resonated as I spoke with other close friends, watched television shows, and listened to the radio. It became clear that many women were feeling the same way. They wanted their vagina back too. They wished that they could find a way to erase bad memories, get rid of diseases they contracted, and eliminate many of the times the gynecologist probed and wrote them prescriptions for creams and pills. But all understood one thing – you can't erase the past, but you can learn from it and make wiser choices in the future.

Then I began to wonder what would happen if after reflecting on their past, women who had some negative feelings about their past sexual behavior would share their stories with others. I wondered if it could prevent one unplanned pregnancy and another woman or girl from raising a child alone in frustration. I wondered if it could prevent some young lady from contracting HIV or spending time and money unnecessarily in a doctor's office to remedy the consequences of her behavior. I wondered if it could minimize the emotional baggage some women carry from being with "the wrong" men. I wondered if it could start a movement.

This book contains stories of everyday women who gave their vagina away, but wished they never did. Its stories are about women who chose to give their vagina away and of those who never had the opportunity to choose if they wanted to give it away.

I Want My Vagina Back is designed to encourage women to share their life stories, but more importantly to assist females (young and not so young) in developing values-driven decisions when it comes to their sexual activities and attitudes.

At the end of each chapter, thought provoking questions challenge the reader to think and share with other women. Strategies for healthy choices are provided in Part II of the book as a way of helping you or others move from past regrets or unhealthy thinking to a future with fewer regrets.

I Want My Vagina Back is for the woman who has learned valuable lessons from past sexual encounters. It is also for the woman who is dealing with physical and emotional issues as a result of sex. Finally, it is for the lady who thinks that she'll never have any regrets about her sexual behavior.

I hope that after reading this book, you will give some thought to your sexual choices and behavior. Whether you're married, single, widowed, or divorced, I hope that you will enjoy reading this book, but more importantly, begin to dialogue with other women and young ladies about how you really feel. I'm hoping that you don't just talk about your sexual experiences, but be candid about the reasons you chose to have sex, the impact it had on your body, what you would do differently if you could do it over again, and why you'd make the decisions you'd make. Please understand that opening up a dialogue about your true feelings can lead to your experiencing unexpected negative emotions. If you find that you're already dealing with or begin to experience feelings of resentment, rage, depression, or thoughts that could lead to unproductive behavior, I strongly suggest that you consult a mental health professional or a trusted spiritual advisor. A trained professional can help you express your feelings in a healthy, productive manner and take steps to resolve those feelings and learn to make choices that won't lead to additional negative emotions and behavior.

For now, sit back with a good cup of tea or water and enjoy taking a peek into the lives of women who might sound like you or someone you know. You're sure to laugh or at least chuckle and reminisce about some of the experiences that only you, the person you were with, and God know about. It'll also challenge you and inspire you to talk to your sister, mother, daughter, friend, and any other female who is important in your life.

Form a group if you have to, but please share, my friend. Your sharing just might help someone else make better decisions. It just might save someone's life and health. It just might keep another woman from having to say like so many of us, "I Want My Vagina Back!"

Table of Contents

PART I

CHAPTER 1

I'D LIKE A REFUND PLEASE

Lady Cia, a woman who has had more partners than she can count tells her story:

Have you ever had sex and felt like "Was that it?" Well that is my story. You know how you can take merchandise back to the store within 30 days and either exchange it or return it as long as you have a receipt? I have had sex a few times when the experience made me want to say, "I tried this and it wasn't what I thought it would be. It looked good while I was looking at it in the mirror, but when I took it home, it didn't fit. I'd like a refund please." I've had other experiences when I felt like I wanted to exchange it for another one that I knew was better.

My problem has been that I have a hard time telling a man that the experience wasn't good. I mean, what do you say when a man says "was it as good for you as it was for me?" If you're like me, you say, "Umm hmmm or oh yeah, it was more than I imagined." All along you're thinking, "He really thinks he just did something, but I could have had more fun watching wall paper dry!"

I've sat back many times and wondered why I kept having sex when I was the one not being satisfied. Especially when my vagina was sore, red, and irritated for a few days from some man who thought that when I said I wanted great sex, it meant rough sex. No, no, no. That's not what great sex is. So why didn't I say something? It was my body, but instead of saying "man, you're hurting me or you're a little too rough", I pretended that I was enjoying it. I know some of you like rough necks who are rough in the bed, but that's something I can do without.

Am I alone or has anyone else had to go and soak to feel better after sex? For the life of me, I really am not sure why I allowed myself to be abused like that. I've apologized to my vagina a few too many times, but I don't think it has ever fully forgiven me or healed. Now that I'm older and value my body, I may be still soaking, but the discount pass to vaginaland is no longer being given to anyone and everyone who wants to sample my goods. I've closed vaginaland. It will only reopen for the man who wants me bad enough to marry me. Until then, no more sales, exchanges or desire for a refund - vaginaland is closed indefinitely.

Vagina poem:

A vagina sale is always final
You can never get a refund or return
Satisfaction is never guaranteed
But from the sale, there are lessons to be learned.

Before you share your vagina
Consider if this is what you want to do
Because once a customer enters vaginaland
You have to live with whatever he does to you.
=====================================

REFLECTION AND DISCUSSION

1. What makes a woman keep silent when she's being hurt or uncomfortable during sexual intercourse?

2. What's the value of your vagina to you?

3. What would you say to a woman who complains that her vagina is often torn, irritated, or bleeding after sex?

CHAPTER 2

IT'S OUR SECRET

Lady B was 15 years old when she had her first sexual encounter. She is 48 now, but remembers it like it was yesterday. Lady B tells her story:

I grew up with 3 brothers. I was the youngest. So as you can imagine, I had a lot of guys in my house all the time.

By the time I was 13, I had the body of an 18 year old woman. Consequently, I got a lot of looks from my brothers' friends. Of course, none of my brothers would let any of their friends come near me. There were a few of them that I was hoping would holla at me, but my brothers would probably hurt them if they did.

Then there was RJ. Oh my goodness. He was fine. He looked so good and when he looked

6

at me, I knew he liked what he saw. But RJ only looked until I turned 15.

RJ was 16 years old and spent many nights at my house. His mother worked the midnight shift and so my mom said it was fine for him to stay with us. Even though RJ was old enough to stay home by himself overnight, he didn't seem to mind coming to our house.

We originally moved into a three bedroom house. After a few years, my parents added a fourth bedroom in the basement for them to sleep in. As the only girl, I had my own room. My two oldest brothers who were away for the summer participating in a study abroad program, shared a room and TC, my 16 year old brother had a room to himself. When RJ came over, he usually slept on one of the bunk beds in TC's room. However, during the summer months while my brothers were in Spain, RJ slept in their room.

Because I thought RJ was so cute, I would sit in the family room with him and my brother TC playing video games or watching sports. Even though my brother would try to make me leave, I would hang out with them until my mother or father told me to let the guys have their time.

One night, during the middle of the summer, days before I turned 16, I was trying to figure out a way to get RJ's attention. I decided to walk out of my bedroom with nothing but my robe on and hopefully give RJ a little peek. Now I had no way of knowing if RJ would be enticed by me, but I was willing to give it a try.

Carefully fixing my robe so that I could quickly conceal myself if my brother looked at me, I walked out of the room toward the kitchen. I noticed that my brother was intensely playing some video game. I stood a few feet from my bedroom for a minute hoping that RJ would turn around, but he seemed to pay me no attention. So I went to the kitchen, got a glass of water and proceeded to walk back to my room. This time, I said "Goodnight bigheads." My brother said "Go to sleep, 'lil girl." RJ turned around and said "Yeah, go to sleep shorty. What you still doing up?" I quickly responded, "both of you can kiss my you know what." Without hesitation, I lifted up my robe and slapped my naked buttocks. Just as I had hoped, RJ was the only one to see my bare skin. Eyebrows lifted, RJ said, "alright, watch yourself girl. You better go to bed before you get a spanking." My brother kept playing the video game without saying a word.

Before closing my bedroom door, I turned to look at RJ. He winked and then nodded his head as if to say, "I want some of that." At that moment, I knew it was just a matter of time.

It was maybe a week or so later before RJ came back over to my house. He and his family went on vacation and had been gone for what seemed like forever. I really wanted to see RJ, but wasn't going to say a word to my brother. I could not stop thinking about RJ. My hormones were raging at the thought of RJ. I don't know why I had such a strong attraction to him. It was as if I would give anything to let him put his hands between my legs. Since I was a virgin, I wasn't so sure that I was ready for sex yet. I think a kiss and a little feel from RJ would be just fine. Even though I knew my mother and my brother would kill me if they knew what I was up to, I could not stop thinking about kissing RJ.

I mentioned to one of my closest friends that there was this guy I was thinking about doing something with, but I never told her his name. Since she had already had sex with a few guys, she egged me on by saying that it was about time I was trying to leave the "virgin club." Every time my friend said that and every time she talked about her sexual escapades, it made sex sound like it was the most pleasurable experience a girl could have. On one hand, I wanted to experience the pleasure my friend described, but on the other hand, I wanted to do what my mother said: "Let your first sexual encounter be with your husband."

The day I had been waiting for finally came. It was a Monday evening around a little past midnight. This was one of those days when my dad had worked a double and was exhausted when he got home. Usually when that happened, he slept like a rock. My mother worked that day and had been doing a bunch of running around so she went to bed before 10 pm. Before going to bed, she told TC and me that RJ's mother would be dropping him off around 11 pm to spend the night.

TC was sitting in the family room when RJ's mother pulled up. He opened the door before RJ could ring the doorbell. After slapping hands to greet one another, RJ walked to the room he usually slept in to drop off his things. He and TC sat in the family room for about an hour before TC said he was tired. RJ told him that he was going to stay up a while and watch a little TV. I only knew this because I sat close to my bedroom door with a glass to hear what was being said.

TC closed the door to his room, and as was customary, turned on his radio which helped him go to sleep a lot faster. Since TC fell asleep pretty quickly, I waited about 15 minutes, put on my robe, walked into the family room, and sat down beside RJ. I don't know what cologne he was wearing, but it was quite sensual. As I sat down, RJ said, "What's happening" and tapped me on my shoulder. "You're what's up, I hope, RJ." Starting to get a little nervous, I started fixing my robe. As if it was planned, instead of pulling my robe together, I pulled one side open and it exposed my left breast. RJ said "Watch it now. Don't start nothin' that you can't finish." Acting like the innocent girl I was, I said "Boy, what do you mean?" "You know what I mean. If you want to tease me, I hope you're trying to please me." Again, playing innocent, I said, "Boy, you know there's no party here. We would both get killed and then there would be a huge conflict between our families if we got caught doing something we shouldn't be doing in my parents' house. Sliding his hand under my robe and rubbing it up and down my leg, RJ said, who says they have to know? This can be our secret. I know you want me."

As if it had been planned, RJ took me by the hand, stood me up and we creeped toward the room he slept in. Before going any further, he stopped at my room, pulled the door shut, and then pulled me down the long hall and into his room. At this point, I was thinking, "This is so wrong. We shouldn't do this. No, this is so wrong." As if he could read my mind, RJ said, "Stop thinking. This is between us. No one needs to know but us. I want you." Just then, he kissed me on my lips. The kiss

12

was so passionate that all I could do was feel my body go limp. I kept thinking, "All I want him to do is feel my vagina, kiss me, and that will be enough. I really should wait. I don't want to do something that I'll regret."

Before I knew it, RJ and I had sex. Although it wasn't what I expected to happen, it was just like my friend said it would be – really good. As I started falling to sleep, RJ whispered, "You'd better go before we both fall asleep." I quickly jumped from the bed while putting on my robe. Although I had just had sex for the first time and enjoyed almost every minute of the experience, I seemed to have this sick feeling on the inside. Before walking out of RJ's room, I turned and said, "I can't believe we just had sex, RJ. Oh my god, please don't tell anyone. I need you to promise that you won't ever tell anyone." With a smile on his face, he jumped out of the bed, came to the door, kissed me on my forehead and said, "This will be our secret. Yeah, our family's dirty little secret."

Thirty-three years have passed and somehow, I haven't been able to get over the fact that I slept with my first cousin. That's right, RJ was my mother's sister's son. He was my mother's favorite nephew.

Sex with RJ continued for about two years until he left to go out of state to college. When I went to a college about 3 hours away from RJ's college, RJ tried to get me to come and see him a few times, but I refused at first. The older I got, the more I realized that what we did was wrong. Six months into our relationship, I started having negative feelings about my relationship with RJ. Still, it didn't stop me from sneaking around to have as much sex with RJ as I could. To hide the shame I was feeling for lying to my parents about me still being a virgin and why I wasn't seeing anyone, I started drinking and taking sleeping pills to help me sleep at night. Nights were when I felt the worst. I couldn't stand to be alone with my thoughts. They haunted me.

RJ and I never told anyone about our relationship. Or at least, I never told and I don't think RJ did either. We both knew that if our family knew about our relationship, it could tear the family apart. For some reason, it never seemed to bother RJ. He acted as if it was normal to sleep with me, his cousin.

After thirty-three years, I'm still an emotional wreck. I've had major depression, gained 45 pounds, and have difficulty being intimate with a man. I think I'm afraid that if I tell a man that I slept with my cousin, he'll think less of me. I also think that I can't get over cousin RJ, my first love and the first male I gave my vagina to. So I drink myself to sleep, eat until I'm comforted, and work long hours to pass the time. And this all started because I wanted my cousin to feel my vagina.

Vagina poem:

I wanted it, had to have it
And look what I got
Now I'm living with a shameful secret
Whether I like it or not
===================================

REFLECTION AND DISCUSSION

1) What are some resources for women who are struggling with the emotional or physical effects of past sexual experiences?

2) Is there anything that Lady B's parents could have done to prevent her from sleeping with her cousin?

3) What could have made it possible for Lady B to tell her family what happened with RJ?

3) If the family secret had been revealed, what could have been done to help everyone deal with it in a healthy, productive manner?

4) Consider sharing with another female what impact sexual experiences you regret have had on you emotionally and how you've dealt with your feelings.

CHAPTER 3

YOU NEVER ASKED ME

Lady B.R., a woman from Alabama shares a story from one of her experiences in college:

I was 21 before I even considered having sex. I grew up in a very religious household where I was told that if I had sex before I got married, I would be condemned to hell. The way my pastor described hell every week during his sermons, it was some place I wanted to avoid. So if having sex would send me there, having sex was not going to happen until I was married.

Well, things didn't go quite that way. After graduating high school, I left home on a scholarship to attend a university in California. Coming from a little town in a small state like Alabama, a big state like California was very exciting, but a little intimidating. I lived on campus, but very quickly made friends with some girls who lived in Los Angeles and commuted to school. Even though my parents checked on me frequently and hounded me about finding a church to attend, I was enjoying my independence and freedom. Finding a church to attend was the last thing on my mind. I had more exciting things to do like go to parties. After my friends convinced me to go to one party, I wanted to go every week and sometimes twice a week.

One Friday night at a fraternity party, I met a guy named El Jay who said he was from a town near my hometown in Alabama. We hit it off almost immediately and started talking on a daily basis.

El Jay was a smooth talker. In addition to being in his junior year of college, he worked part-time selling marketing and promotional items. That brother could sell air if he wanted. I saw him make a few sales on campus using his charm and good looks.

From the time El Jay and I started getting close, I told him that I was not ready to engage in sexual intercourse. So if he wanted to have sex, he should think about being with someone else. El Jay insisted that he was a gentleman and would not try to pressure me into having sex.

El Jay and I were several months into our relationship and things were going really well. I felt good whenever I was with El Jay, like I could trust him. Not once did he try to have sex with me. All we ever did was kiss and when things started getting a little heated, El Jay was always the one to pull away. I think if El Jay had asked me to have sex, I might have agreed. I felt like I was falling in love with him and was willing to let him be my first even if he didn't end up being my husband. Still, El Jay never asked.

One evening, El Jay invited me to attend one of his fraternity parties. Some guys had just finished pledging and the fraternity brothers were throwing a big party for them at the fraternity house. El Jay asked if some of my friends and I would come to the fraternity house around 11 p.m. That, he said, would give the brothers enough time to go through some formalities with the neophytes. Since it was a Saturday night and I enjoyed spending time with El Jay, I agreed to come by.

I called two of my closest friends and asked them to go with me to the party. Both agreed. We arrived at the fraternity house around 11:15pm. The party was jumping when we got there. There had to be about 200 people in the house. We were packed in there like sardines.

El Jay was near the bar when I arrived. When he spotted me, he came over and gave me a big hug and kiss and pulled me onto the dance floor. We must have danced 5 or 6 records before I asked for something to drink. El Jay came back with a mixed drink that I never tasted before. I still don't know what it was, but it was delicious and quenched my thirst.

It was 3:00 a.m. when I woke up and realized I was in El Jay's bed with nothing on but my bra. Shocked and feeling a little lightheaded, I shook El Jay who lay next to me on top of the covers snoring. He was completely naked. After shaking him a few times with no response, I shouted as loud as I could. "El Jay, what happened? What happened El Jay? How did I get in your bed and why are my clothes off? Disoriented from being abruptly awakened, El Jay said, "Go back to sleep babe. We'll talk about it in a few hours. I'm out of it." "El Jay, No! We have to talk about it NOW! I want to know what happened." El Jay tried to calm me down by pulling me close to him. I'm sure he didn't want me to wake up his roommate or anyone else who was in the frat house. "Stop it, El Jay. I need to know what happened. You know I am, I mean, yes, I am a virgin. So you have to talk to me NOW, El Jay. Wiping saliva from the corners of his mouth, El Jay said "Calm down. Nothing happened that you didn't ask for." What do you mean El Jay? What do you mean, nothing happened that I DIDN'T ASK FOR? What did I ask for? With a big smile, El Jay began to fill me in. "Babe, you had a few drinks. Then you started getting a little freaky. I was getting upset at first, but then you were turning me on. So I just let you do your thing. You were having so much fun." In disbelief, I shouted, "Getting freaky? I don't get freaky. What are you talking about? I don't remember doing anything freaky." "That's probably cuz the liquor had you free for real, babe. I liked you like that."

With tears coming to my eyes, I started beating El Jay on his chest. "So what did I do El Jay? Why I am in your bed with only a bra on?" Smiling a little bigger, but seeing how upset I was, El Jay looked me in the eyes and said, "Sweetheart, you gave me something I've never had, but wanted." Sobbing uncontrollably, with a shaky voice, I said, "You took my virginity, El Jay while I was intoxicated. Is that what you did? And now you're trying to act like I gave it to you. You never asked me if I would have sex with you, El Jay. You know how I felt about having sex with you. I didn't want to and now you've taken that away from me!" "No, baby, it wasn't like that at all. You gave it willingly. You were the one who started dancing sexy with one of my friends. I tried to stop you, but then you pulled me close to you and started dancing real sexy with both of us. Then you started rubbing on both of us and whispered in my ear that you wanted to leave. At first I said no because I thought it was the liquor talking, but you insisted. You said you wanted me to take you home and make love to you. So you gave it to me babe or should I say you gave it to us. "Us?" Yes, girl. You gave me what I've been wanting for a long time. You had sex with my boy and me, and then we took turns performing oral sex on you while my boy and I had sex. That's what you gave me - a threesome."

Vagina poem:

He took it and that ain't right
Just to do what he wanted one night
It's called rape and he needs to pay
For deciding to take my virginity away
==================================

REFLECTION AND DISCUSSION

1) Date rape occurs too often amongst college students. What are some things that you've done to prevent yourself from being in a situation like this?

2) El Jay never told Lady B.R. of his desire to have sex with another man. What conversations do females need to have with males they're interested in in order to get to know them better?

3) What would you share with a woman who told you that she was asked to participate in "a threesome"?

4) With an increasing number of couples engaging in swinging and open relationships, what would you say are some things a female might consider before agreeing having sex with more than one person at the same time?

CHAPTER 4

THE COST OF NO LIMIT LOVE

Once you've shared your vagina with someone, it's not like you can ask for it back and get it. What's done is done. Not only do you have to deal with the memories of the experience (good, bad, or worst), there are times when your mind, body, and soul pay the price for moments of intimacy.

Lady T.W. shares her story

I got married right out of college. My husband GJ graduated from college two years before me and was working as a computer programmer for the federal government.

GJ and I dated for three years before we got married. During those three years, our sex life was hot and heavy. We had sex at least 5 times a week and sometimes three times a day. We couldn't seem to get enough of each other. After we got married, things were about

25

the same for about 5 years. GJ's job started requiring him to travel to field offices at least 3 times a month. He traveled at least 10-15 days some months. I didn't mind at first because when GJ returned from each trip, we would try to make up for lost time. I was in love with my husband and had no doubt he was in love with me.

GJ came home from work one day and said that he had been assigned to travel to 15 additional sites over the next 10 months and might have to be gone 15-20 days out of the month. There was a major project that his agency was behind on and needed his expertise to meet one of the contract's deliverables within the next 12 months.

GJ was excited about this opportunity because he would be receiving a pay increase and would be going to some states and countries he had never visited.

I was less excited because I would be seeing my sweetheart a lot less. But I decided that instead of getting frustrated, I would find something to do with my time. I also would travel with him or visit him when I could get off.

For the first month or so, whenever my husband was gone, I visited family and friends after work and on the weekends. I think I started wearing out my welcome. Then one day, I decided to go to one of the area gyms and get in the pool. Working as a part-time trainer was this sexy brother that caught my attention right away, but not enough for me to really be interested. After about a week of going to the gym, somehow, my feelings had changed. The trainer and I had a lot in common so we talked incessantly for hours or until the gym closed. Eventually, I gave him my number and we talked every night and some mornings before I went to work.

The bottom line is that we started having an affair. I thought sex with my husband was off the hook but Raymond, the trainer, did things to me I never knew could be done. What started out as a one time event became a habit. I was like a crack addict chasing the ghost. I couldn't get enough of my lover's loving. Since he was single, he was available

27

almost anytime I called and you can believe I called often. My husband was consumed by his work and didn't seem to have a clue what was going on. Although the frequency of sex between us declined significantly, we both blamed it on how tired he was and how often he was out of town.

Everything seemed to be going fine until I got really sick one evening while my husband was home and had to go to the emergency room. My temperature reached 104.3 and the doctors couldn't figure out what was causing it to be so high. After running a series of tests, one of the doctors came to my bedside and said, "Well I have some news for you that may explain your high fever. M'aam, it seems that you have a bacterial infection." Relieved to know what was wrong and that it could be treated, I relaxed on the bed as my husband kissed me on the lips and forehead. He had been so worried. As he looked me in the eyes and said "I love you", the doctor said "One more thing. The results of the tests also showed that you tested positive for HIV."

My husband immediately flung my hand to the bed and screamed "Say what? Doc, what did you just…Did you just say HIV?" What the….? Babe, what does he mean HIV? How in the hell did you contract HIV? You surely didn't get it from me. No, forget this. I don't even want to hear a response. There's nothing you can tell me 'cuz I know it didn't come from me."

Although I tried and the doctors and nurses tried to calm my husband down, he was irate. Security came and he tried to fight them. My husband was livid and probably would have hurt something or someone if they hadn't detained him. I was shocked, hurt, ashamed, and embarrassed. I couldn't believe that Raymond had given me HIV. For a split second, I wondered if it was possible that my husband gave it to me, but I quickly dismissed the thought. I knew it had to be Raymond. I was angry and wanted to get out of bed and go hurt Raymond, but I also wanted to hurt myself for getting involved with him. How could he do this to my husband and me? How could he knowingly infect me? So many thoughts ran through my head until I was physically and emotionally exhausted. But I was too distraught to go to sleep. I don't even know what the doctor said after he gave me the diagnosis. I know they wanted to keep me for observation because my blood count was very low. In the hospital was probably the best place for me, but I didn't like being there alone.

My husband left me only hours after hearing my diagnosis. Two days later when I arrived to our home, my husband had removed almost everything except my clothes, a few dishes and towels, and our bed. He even took the car he purchased for me.

For weeks, my husband refused to answer my calls and his family shunned me. It was one of the worst times in my life. To add insult to injury, what the doctor hadn't gotten around to telling me during all of the commotion was that I was pregnant.

I was miserable for the next few months. In addition to morning sickness, I was on all kinds of medication. I wanted to get an abortion, but I couldn't make myself do it. I was so confused and experienced bouts of depression. Raymond called me a few times, but I refused to talk with him. I didn't know what to say. At times I wanted him to come and make everything ok, but I would soon remember that it was because of him that my life was a mess. Well, I knew that I chose to have unprotected sex with Raymond, but I never thought I would contract HIV. I guess that was the problem – I wasn't thinking.

I cried myself to sleep most nights. I wanted everything to be back to the way it was before I started having an affair with Raymond. If I could just turn back the hands of time, I would not allow myself to get involved with Raymond or anyone else. It hadn't been worth it. Now I had to live with HIV, carry a baby and not know which of the two men the father of my child was, and deal with the guilt, shame, and hurt that I'd caused.

I eventually lost the house and had to move back home with my parents. My husband filed for an absolute divorce and from what I heard, had accepted a position in another state. Hearing that news caused me to realize my life would never be the same because I chose to share my vagina with a man who didn't deserve it and who decreased its value significantly. I not only wanted my vagina back from Raymond, I needed it back!

Vagina poem:

When loving you is wrong, I don't want to be wrong. The price that I will pay just to play with someone else's emotions ain't worth being with Mr. Jones. We'll just have to have a thing going on in another life when loving him is right.
======================================

REFLECTION AND DISCUSSION

1) What leads to a woman deciding to have sex with a man when she is married?

2) What consequences have you suffered as a result of sharing your vagina with someone who shouldn't have been given an access pass?

3) If you could put an access code with terms and conditions on your vagina, what would the terms and conditions be?

4) What would you say to a woman who is contemplating having an affair, who is in an extramarital relationship, or is having sex with multiple partners?

CHAPTER 5

DON'T LET YOUR VAGINA

BE YOUR GUIDE

Our values frequently guide our behavior. Unfortunately, too often, we allow our feelings to guide what we do. That may work out well in some cases, but in many cases, our feelings can lead us to a life full of regrets and apologies. This is true especially when it comes to sex.

A number of religions teach that you are expected to abstain from sex until you are married. Your husband is to be the person who breaks the hymen – or what I'll call, the safety seal over the entrance to your vagina. Like a covering on a new bottle of jelly, an unbroken seal is supposed to be an indication that the product is safe and has not been tampered with. When the seal has been broken when you purchase the product, it is a sign that the product may have been tampered with and may be damaged or poisoned goods.

Over the years, men share that they love to be a girl or woman's "first". What do women say? Have you been told that your body is special and that it shouldn't be shared with just anyone? Let me ask another question: Why is it that females share their body much quicker than they will some of their personal belongings?

For many years, I've posed the following question to teens and young adults: If you just met someone, would you take off your gold, silver, or platinum necklace and give it to him/her? Most of the time, 99% of the people do one of a few things: 1) look at me like I've lost my mind; 2) respond with a definitive NO or 3) a combination of 1 and 2. I then say, "So why is it that you can meet someone for the first time and give him/her your body to do whatever is desired? Young ladies and men come up with all kinds of reasons. "Well that's different." To which I respond, "So you're saying that the value of your necklace or ring or your car or some other prized possession is greater than the value of your body?" The response is almost always the same – NO.

Many females don't recognize the worth of their body. Many don't understand that wear and tear on the body can reduce its "shelf life" and lead to lots of maintenance.

They don't understand that early sexual activity, especially with multiple partners can lead to them contracting venereal diseases including HPV, herpes, and HIV/AIDS and put them at high risk of developing cervical cancer.

What are astounding are the risk-taking behaviors of some females. Some are willing to play all kinds of games and participate in all sorts of sexual acts without fear of or serious concern for the consequences of risky behavior.

About four or five years ago, I read an article that described a group of teens whose risky behavior had been exposed by one of the group members and her counselor. Apparently, the teens would frequent a home in a suburban community and play sex games. One of the games involved oral sex. Each girl who was willing to participate in the game chose a different color lip gloss, put it on her lips and went into one of the bedrooms. With all of the girls in the room, one by one, each boy would enter the room. The object of the game was to see which boy could get the most colors of lipstick on his penis.

In addition to oral sex, this group of teens was said to be participating in "threesomes" and used all types of sex toys with and on one another. They had weekly sex parties. When interviewed by a counselor, some of the teens said they didn't see anything wrong with their behavior. They felt like they could be doing worse things like drinking, using drugs, or committing crimes. They believed they knew what they were doing and wasn't hurting anyone because each teen knew what the other was doing. There was no deception and no crime.

When is the last time you had a serious conversation with your son, daughter, younger sister, niece, nephew, or others close to you about making responsible decisions when it comes to sex? Do you really care about the next generation of youth and their sexual behavior?

One of the things I have prided myself on is being able to have very candid conversations with my children over the years. We didn't talk about everything, but when it came to sex, they knew what I desired for them and knew that I wanted them to make responsible choices. Not only did I talk with my daughter about valuing her body, but expressed to my son the seriousness of having sex. I shared with him some of the challenges females have long after males have wiped off, zipped up their pants, and gone on about their business. Even though my son didn't like to hear about yeast infections and the probing of the gynecologist, I felt it was important for him to have an understanding of the impact he could have on a female's body. I also shared some of the consequences of my sexual behavior and the ways I had to deal with those consequences many years after the sexual acts occurred. Their dad did the same thing. He had very candid and sometimes graphic conversations with our children.

To say that my children have been perfect would be telling an outright lie. However, regardless of what they may or may not have done, I felt it was my responsibility to give them wise information that they could use to make decisions. To this day, I have a very close relationship with my adult children. We have candid, open conversations about many things including sex. Even though I have not always liked some things they have shared with me, I appreciate our relationship and their willingness to consult me on some difficult topics.

Vagina poem:

My body says yes, my mind says no
I see a green light, which way should I go?
==================================

REFLECTION AND DISCUSSION

1) When is the last time you talked with a female you care about, about the value of her body?

2) How aware are you of the risk taking behavior of the females (e.g., friends, relatives, students, mentees) in your life?

3) What are some things you can do and say to help young girls and women value their body much more than physical possessions and other people?

4) Discuss your thoughts about having "friends with benefits". Specifically, what should females be aware of when choosing to have casual sexual relationships with one or more partners?

CHAPTER 6

WHEN YOUR CHILD CRIES, SHE MIGHT NEED YOU!

After years of hiding her pain, Lady P has learned how much her past sexual experiences affected her for more than 30 years. Lady P tells her story:

I was molested as a young child. The fondling of my vagina awakened something in me that I didn't quite know what to do with. Consequently, in addition to drinking, smoking, and getting high, I became sexually active before I was a teenager. During the end of my 13th year, I got pregnant by a guy who was 4 years my senior. When my parents learned of my pregnancy, I was almost in my 16th week.

Since I was only 13 years old, even though I wanted to carry my child to full-term, arrangements were made for me to have an abortion in a local hospital. I was given a saline injection. Basically, a long needle was injected into my stomach which ultimately killed the baby and induced my labor. At that point, the labor continued until my body ejected a dead child. I was in labor for at least six hours. It was such a horrible and painful experience for me. I probably won't forget it as long as I live.

After my dead son was shown to me, I counted his fingers and toes, stared at him with remorse, and cried. Alone with a dead child and a nurse in a hospital room a little after midnight, I was traumatized. This experience sent me into a depression and into a spiral of destructive behavior.

Eventually, my boyfriend started seeing someone else. My dad threatened to have him sent to jail if he came around me anymore. At that point, I tried to commit suicide several times. I couldn't handle the grief, rejection, and shame. I took a handful of pain pills which caused me to become extremely drowsy and eventually fall asleep. Fortunately, I woke up each time I took the pills, but with the thought that I wished I hadn't.

In addition to being distraught over the breakup and the abortion, my boyfriend questioned whether I had really been pregnant or if it had been a ploy to get some money from him. I had no one to talk to about what was swimming around in my head. I was drowning in my pain and felt like no one noticed. That may not have been true, but that's how I was feeling.

I began to wear an array of masks to hide my pain. I learned how to become an excellent actress while wearing a mask that only I knew was on.

My grief and pain turned into resentment. So I vowed to never allow another man hurt me like my former boyfriend did. I made up my mind that I would become the cheater, the one who hurt others, and the one who would never get hurt by a man again.

I ended up being in more relationships than I can remember. I used sex like a hobby and wouldn't allow any male to get too close.

During my teen years, I dated multiple guys at the same time and was good for doing a "wham, bam, thank ya man" on them. I didn't care about self respect, value, or the consequences of my actions. I just did whatever eased my pain and kept me from living in a dark, unhappy place.

Over the years, I've had many other traumatic experiences. From being raped to being in car accidents and an elevator accident, to having a number of different surgeries and having men cheat on me with friends and church members. I have been through an emotional ringer. Among other things, sex continued to be my drug of choice, my exercise, and the weapon I used to control and manipulate some of the men in my life. I even prostituted myself with a few private clients. If I needed some money and they wanted the sex, if I could pick up the phone and make the arrangement, we had a deal. Well, let me put it another way: I'd call and ask for a little financial assistance. The response was usually, sure, but you'll have to come and get it or meet me somewhere. It was understood that I would be given money in exchange for sex. Like I said, I prostituted myself.

The consequences of my sexual behavior left me visiting or calling my gynecologist more times than I care to remember. I've had other abortions, venereal diseases, a level III Pap smear, countless yeast infections, and all sorts of stuff that itched, burned, smelled, and appeared in a variety of colors and textures. I've popped pills, been given a shot, had my uterus frozen, inserted all types of creams into my vagina, popped all kinds of pills and eventually had my uterus removed.

I went through all of this because I used my vagina like it was an ice-cream truck that called out "Come and get it." Having sex with different men left me emotionally and physically sick and cost me a lot of money for things my insurance didn't cover. As you can imagine, there are a bunch of doors that if I could, I'd go back and say "I want my vagina back, right now." As a matter of fact, I think I'd even be willing to pay to get it back if I could!

More importantly, I've become sensitive to the cries of young ladies and encourage mothers and other women to pay attention to the behavior of the women around them. When young ladies act out, it's important to consider what's going on. In many cases, females are crying for attention. Their behavior is merely a symptom of some things they haven't communicated to you in words. In some cases, they may not have the words to express what they're feeling or they might not understand the ways sexual or other experiences might be affecting them. Unfortunately, we observe negative behavior, make judgments, use negative reinforcement, and never help young ladies deal with what's really going on to cause them to act inappropriately. That causes them to keep on a mask and continue to express hurt, anger, or depression. So the next time you see a young lady acting out, remember it might be her way of crying for help. Most importantly, if she acts out in your presence or while in your care, it's possible that she's crying for you.

Vagina poem:

A child is molested, it awakens something
inside
But she doesn't know who to tell, so her
feelings she hides
A child will become a woman, still scarred
from her past
She will look for ways to make her life move
really fast.

The girl uses sex to ease her pain
She keeps crying, but no one hears and no
one sees her stains
That little girl continues to cry until someone
shows her the way
Look around and help the little girl stop crying
Or she'll become a woman whose skies are
always grey.
=====================================

REFLECTION AND DISCUSSION

Children who are molested are likely to act out unless and until support (and in some cases, ongoing support) is provided to help them deal with what was done to them. Children need an outlet to express their feelings. Unfortunately, in some cases, they will internalize their feelings especially when they're uncertain that anyone will believe them. They also may fear that nothing will be done or that something else will be done to them for telling on the perpetrator. In many cases, children and adolescents who have been molested act out in ways that are not age appropriate or "normal."

1) Everyone has a story to tell. If you had to describe the faces of women you know who have experienced molestation, rape, or incest and who have not received counseling or other support to help them deal with the traumatic experiences, how would you describe them?

2) Are you carrying secrets about yourself or others that affect the way you live your life? If

yes, consider seeking out a mental health professional that can help you talk about your secrets and come to some resolve.

What resources can you share to help girls or women who have experienced molestation, rape, incest, or other types of negative sexual experiences?

3) How has your sexual behavior affected your physical and emotional health?

4) If you could do it over, would you give your virginity away to the same person or would you have waited? Why or why not?

CHAPTER 7

THE BEST PERFORMANCE IS THE ONE WE PERFORM TOGETHER

Lady Shaw says that she saved herself until marriage. Lady Shaw tells her story:

Girl, over the years I've heard many sayings about how you can tell what you're going to get in the bedroom. Some said it was the motion in the ocean, whatever that means. Others said it was the size and length of his fingers or his feet. Other women said it was the way he moves his body on the dance floor. I have spent so much time looking at a man's hands, feet, the bulge in his pants, and how he moved on the dance floor. What I've come to realize is that none of that stuff really matters. Now that I'm old and have been married for 45 years, I know that it's not what he's got, but what you teach him to do with it to meet your needs.

Unlike many women, I was still a virgin at the age of 29 when I married my husband. My mother made me think that sex was something dirty and extremely painful. When I was growing up, we lived in a two-bedroom house. My bedroom was right next to my parents. So I'd occasionally hear them in their room doing something, which I now know was having sex, but it sounded painful. I ran out of my room a few times and knocked on their door to make sure they were ok. My dad would yell and tell me everything was fine and to go back to bed. When I would ask my mother the next morning if she was ok, she would tell me that she was having a few pains in her body and my dad was helping to ease the pain. She never said that she and my dad were doing something beautiful and that the sounds I was hearing were expressions of the pleasure. No, she made it seem like she had chronic pain. But when I asked her about sex, she would always say that it's something that hurts, gets you all messy, then makes your stomach swell and hurt for hours. As you can imagine, I was not trying to do anything that would lead to such pain and torment.

I went through college and graduate school believing what my mother said. Friends told me a lot of things about sex, but nothing could change my reality. Sex was only something I would do when I got married and was ready to have children. Even when I dated a guy and he would kiss me and start fondling me a little, I would never go any further even though what he did felt really good. I kept thinking that maybe that was the only good part. At times when a guy started fondling me, I would feel a little pain in my vagina and would quickly push him away.

After I got married, friends of mine and I began to have many conversations about our love lives. Unlike me, my friends were quite uninhibited and had sex with a number of guys prior to getting married. One thing I noticed was that they all seemed to compare their husband's sexual behavior to someone from their past. They compared the size of his penis, foreplay, whether he talked or didn't talk during sex, what kind of noises he made, how long he took to ejaculate, how well he performed oral sex, if he performed oral sex, and whether or not he seemed to be in it for himself or to please his wife.

I felt so inexperienced every time we had those conversations. After all, I had no one to compare my husband to. He was my one and only. My friends, on the other hand, had either been divorced once or twice, had an affair, or were longing for the experience they had with someone other than their husbands.

Our "girl talk" helped me realize how dissatisfied my friends were because they were still trying to experience what they had in the past. Because one man made her "see stars", one of my friends was always looking for that magical moment with her husband. Because she didn't experience that, she complained about her husband all the time and expressed to us how sexually frustrated she was. "It's like watching a bad movie for the 100th time when he's so called making love to me. It is the most boring thing I've ever experienced."

All of my close friends said they faked orgasms just to get sex over with. I couldn't imagine being so deceptive, but then again, I wondered if I would be like my friends if I had more experience. Either way, it helped me appreciate my relationship with my husband even more.

One day I shared with my friends that I had a wonderful sex life with my husband. Over the years, we showed each other how to keep one another satisfied. After I got over what my mother told me, I found the experience to be wonderful. Even though our sex drives had diminished, at 74 and 75 years old, we still occasionally had sex and did other things to keep each other satisfied. My friends, who were 5-10 years younger, were astonished. They couldn't believe that after 45 years, I only had one lover and continued to enjoy our times of intimacy.

I asked my friends if they thought their thinking about sex needed to change. I believed that if they thought differently about sex, their level of satisfaction might increase. I explained that if they stopped thinking about what previous partners did, they might learn to enjoy what they have and possibly end up having sexual experiences far greater than anything they could imagine.

What I have come to understand is that there are a lot of memories that go along with sharing your vagina with men. Some may be good memories, but they can influence your expectations of the man you ultimately commit to. Here's an analogy that I've shared with my friends: What if you went to school and your performance was constantly being measured against someone who took the class prior to you and who you didn't know? And what if the teacher did not provide you with any support or instructions? He just kept letting you perform, kept complaining about your level of performance, and talked about what he was used to. What if he did this behind your back, but would tell you how good of a job you were doing? That would be unfair to you because you wouldn't know that your performance needed improving and what you could do to make it better. It would help if he told you your performance needed to improve or at least give you feedback and offer you suggestions on how to have peak performance. If the teacher wants you to perform to a certain standard, rather than comparing you to a former student, it would be fair if he let you know how to perform to standard.

It's the same way with sex. When you keep comparing and complaining about a man's performance, you're suggesting that his performance is based solely on what he does and that you don't play a part in making the experience whatever you desire it to be.

I know you can't go and get your vagina back, but at least work on letting the memories of past sexual experiences stay in the past so that you can be present and make the most of the experiences with the man you've chosen to share your life and body with.

====================================

REFLECTION AND DISCUSSION

1) What do you view as the purpose of sex?

2) What are some of the benefits of abstinence?

3) Some people believe that intimacy and sex are the same or that they go hand-in-hand. What do you believe? What are the benefits of intimacy with or without sex?

4) Talk with an older woman (65+) about sex or a woman who has been in a relationship without sex due to age, physical or other conditions. Ask if her view of sex has changed over time and how to exist in a relationship when there's no sex.

CHAPTER 8

NO ONE TAUGHT ME

HOW TO SAY NO

How many times have you found yourself in an awkward situation and wanted to say no, but you went along with whatever you were being asked to do? For instance, what happens when you're in a room with a man who you have an interest in? In the moment, he kisses you. Ahhh that was a nice kiss. Now he begins to pull you closer and hold you tighter. At this point, you may not even think about how comforting it feels. Then he starts to undress you. "Hold up, wait a minute", you think. "I was ok with him kissing me, but this is the second date and I'm not comfortable having sex with him." As if he could read your mind, he says: "I want you so bad, but it's ok if you don't want me. Oh, I want you baby......" The next thing you know, your clothing is off and this man is on top of you thrusting his

58

penis inside of you. Right before he entered your vagina, you wanted to say no, but didn't.

What makes women and girls lose their voice when it comes to engaging in sexual acts? Some would suggest that it's low self esteem and the desire for males to have a certain perception of them. Others suggest that females get caught up in a male's charm and his ability to say all of the right things.

What do you think? Why do some women give power over to a man when they want to say no and have the ability and power to say no? You've heard the stories. From the rape cases in the news involving famous men to the countless women who complain that sex is bad but repeatedly go back to have sex with the same man, some women don't act as if saying no is an option.

Some women say that if they say no, men might leave for another woman who will say yes. Other women say that bad sex is better than no sex. Others say that they're supposed to keep their men satisfied. One woman claimed that whenever she said no, her man would begin kissing her, pick her up if necessary, throw her down on the bed, couch or floor, and force his way into her. Because they were in a relationship, she didn't view this as rape. She saw it as part of the relationship. She believed that this was his way of expressing how bad he wanted "her stuff."

Days before dying, Claire wrote the following letter to her daughter, Sheryl:

Dear Baby Girl,

I'm sorry that I never had the chance to have this conversation with you. If I had known that my life would end this way, I would have talked with you a long time ago. Forgive me for not being the mother to you that I should have been. I have been a terrible example for you and I pray that what I share in this letter will keep you from behaving like me.

Sheryl, I became a prostitute when I was 17 years old. That's all I've ever known. I have slept with more men than I can count or remember. They have done some things to me that I never wanted to share with anyone until now. Baby, I allowed men to insert objects into my body. One had a pet gerbel that he forced into my rectum. Even though that thing nibbled and tore my rectum, I hollered, but let that man do whatever he wanted as long as he paid me my fee. Then there was the one guy who paid me to perform oral sex on 15 guys pledging his fraternity. I was even hired to sleep with women and their boyfriends or husbands.

I've been beaten and left to die a few times. But each time, the man I belonged to, my pimp, would find me, blame me for doing something wrong, and make me go back to work as soon as I looked half-way presentable. Baby girl, at one point the doctor told me if I had sex again before I allowed my body to heal, that I could do irreparable damage to the inner walls of my vagina. Still, I had no choice but go back on the streets. That's all I knew until you came into my life.

From the day I laid eyes on you, I knew that you would be something special. I wanted to protect you, but I couldn't. For that, I gotta tell you I'm sorry. I never meant for those men to do what they did to you. I tried to stop them,

I Want My Vagina Back

but I needed my drugs and they paid me as long as I allowed them to have sex with you. At first I didn't feel bad, especially since you were 12, but I knew it was wrong. Even in the condition I was in, I knew it was wrong. I'm so sorry that I did that to you.

Baby girl, I don't know if I would have gotten into that life if it hadn't been for my uncle and my mother. From the time I was seven, my uncle made me have sex with him a bunch of times. He taught me how to make money with my body. Every time I had sex with him, he gave me $10. He always told my mom that he was giving me money, but never told her the truth. He just said that I was his favorite niece and he wanted to give me a few dollars that I could save or spend on something that I wanted. My mom never told me to say NO. Then when I was 15 and I told her that the owner of the store tried to hit on me, my mom told me not to say anything bad to him. That if he was willing to give us something free from the store, to flirt with him a little. She never told me to say NO to his advances. So just like my mom had said, I flirted with the store owner. Then one day he called me into the back of the store into a little room and closed the door. He raped me, then told me to take some groceries home to my mother. I ran out of the store without the groceries and went home to tell my mother what happened. She looked at me and asked where the groceries were. Believe it or not, mom sent me back to the store the next week to see if the store owner would give me the groceries he was going to give me. You probably already guessed that if I went to get the groceries, the owner would expect me to have sex with him. That would make him happy, mom would be happy, and it would teach me that I didn't have a voice.

Sheryl, I ran away from home when I was 16. I left after my mother tried to get me to sleep with her boyfriend. She did that after he told her that was the only way he would pay the rent for that month. That's how I ended up on the streets as a prostitute.

I'm dying baby girl. The doctor said it's just a matter of time before I take my last breath. I'm so weak that I dictated this letter to one of the nurses.

I'm so sorry that I wasn't a better mother. There's so much about my life that I regret. I wish I could take back every sexual act that was done to me. I wish I could erase every disease and surgery I had. I wish I could stop every man and woman from satisfying themselves and making me satisfy them at my expense.

Please promise me that you will never sell your body to anyone. Promise me that you won't hate me for who I was and what was done to you. Promise me that you will say no when you want to; that you'll say no when someone doesn't want you to say no; and say no for all of the times that your mother didn't. No one taught me how to say no, Sheryl. I hope in my dying that you will find your voice. I hope my letter will always be a reminder that although I may not have taught you much, I wanted to teach you how to say NO, baby girl. I'm not asking for anything else, Sheryl. Just promise me that you'll learn to say NO!

Please don't forget me, Sheryl. Please forgive me. I really am sorry. Yes, I was a sorry mother, but I apologize and hope you can forgive me and learn to say no. I want my vagina back, Sheryl, but it's much too late. The cancer has destroyed my body and my vagina is worthless. Learn to say no, Sheryl. Say no so that you won't wish you could get your vagina back like me, your mother.

Love,

Claire, your Mom.

====================================

REFLECTION AND DISCUSSION

1) How have you felt when you said or demonstrated a yes when you really wanted to say no to sex? Why?

2) What can you do to help another female who uses her body to make a living and wants out of that lifestyle before it destroys her?

3) What message do you have for a woman who has lost her voice and can't seem to say no when asked to have sex?

CHAPTER 9

HE'LL LEAVE HER FOR ME

What do you call a woman who has sex with another woman's husband? If I ask 20 different women that same question, I'd probably get at least 10 different answers.

There used to be a time when there was a respect for marriage. Even though there were single women who had affairs with married men and other women who kept a "sugar daddy" on the side, there was a perception that women did not feel comfortable having an affair with another woman's husband. There was the belief that it was disrespectful to the wife and to the marriage contract or covenant.

If you turn on the television, radio, or internet, you're bound to hear stories of affairs. What I find interesting is that some women don't feel there's anything wrong with having sex with a married man. Some women say that as long as the married man takes care of their needs, helps with bills, and doesn't require much of their time, they're alright with the relationship. When asked how they feel about the wife, some women indicate that they don't allow themselves to think too much about the wife. Others say they simply don't care – that if the wife was taking care of business, her husband wouldn't be stepping out on her to get his needs met somewhere else.

Depending on your values, beliefs, and culture, this behavior may seem quite inappropriate and disgusting. Others might find it acceptable and have compelling reasons why it is acceptable.

Regardless of how you feel about women being involved with married men, there are some lessons to be learned from this type of relationship.

Take Rose for instance. She agrees with others that if she could get her vagina back from the married men she slept with, she would walk, drive, or catch a bus to go pick it up.

Here's Rose's story:

I grew up around a lot of divorced women. I heard a lot of negative talk about marriage. My mom and her five sisters constantly told stories about cheating husbands, the "other women", and how men were only good for sex and money. They often said that the only thing you could depend on a man for was an erect penis.

Hearing these messages caused me to develop distrust for men and believe that there would always be another woman in the picture for every man I dated. I just didn't think that any man was trustworthy. When I started dating, I had in my mind that the best men to date were the married ones. Since like my mom and aunts, I believed men were only good for sex and money, I wasn't looking for a long-term relationship, just men to meet my physical and financial needs.

I tried dating single men at first, but they proved to be just like the married ones – cheaters. So I figured I might as well be involved with married men. At least they wouldn't be around all the time and they came with some good benefits.

I was 20 when I first got into a relationship with a married man named Paul. Paul was 45 years old and claimed to be in the process of separating from his wife. He gave me a personal credit card to shop with and helped me pay the rent on my one bedroom apartment. Paul said he'd continue to give me money and allow me to use the credit card as long as I didn't have sex with anyone else and didn't do anything to mess things up between him and his wife. After all, he was in the process of getting her to agree to a separation and divorce and he didn't want to give her a reason to ask for alimony.

At times, Paul was controlling and when we had sex, he liked to role play. I won't even talk about some of the roles he wanted me to play. I cringe every time I think about what I used to do to satisfy that man.

After several years of being in a relationship with Paul, I wanted us to be together. I was in love with Paul. He promised me that we would be together and for me to be patient. Four years later, Paul was still living with his wife and I wanted more out of our relationship than he could give me.

Instead of ending the relationship with Paul, I started going out with Louis, another married man. I told Louis that I was dating another man, but would be ending that relationship. Louis, who was 22 years older than me, said he understood. We only saw each other when he wanted to have sex. I was ok with it at first because the sex was really good, but soon realized that other than sex, there were no benefits.

Louis would come over early in the morning to have sex before going to work or would have me come to his office in the evenings so his wife thought he was working. He would even call her from his office with me present.

Still in a relationship with Paul, I was getting tired of dealing with two married men. I was also afraid that if Paul found out about Louis he would stop paying my bills and take away my credit card. I was working, but had now purchased a home with Paul's help of course. I felt as if I had to stay with Paul. Otherwise, I couldn't pay my bills. So I stayed in a relationship with Paul for 10 more years.

I ended up having three children by Paul. He has taken care of them, but at times, has treated me like a lowlife prostitute. As you probably already know, Paul never left his wife. As a matter of fact, after Paul's wife found out about me and Paul's three children, she contacted me and said she had no intention of divorcing her husband and that my child support payments would come through her.

Even though I continued to let Paul come over and have sex with me, I grew to resent him and now felt like I was justified in feeling like my mom and sisters – that men were only good for sex and money. I believed that they lied, were manipulative, and were self-serving. Despite these feelings, I continued to give in to his lies – the one that he really loved me; the one that he really wanted to be with me, but if he left his wife, it might make her heart condition worse; and the one that he had so much respect for me because I was a strong woman who showed him the meaning of unconditional love. Despite Paul cancelling my credit card and only giving me a few dollars here and there, child support was all I could count on from Paul. Call me crazy, but I continued to believe that Paul and I would be together some day.

It has been 30 years since I first started dating Paul. Our children are grown and have children of their own. Paul died two years ago of cancer. I wasn't able to visit him in the hospital and his wife warned me that things would get ugly if I came to Paul's funeral.

Paul left me just as he found me – broke, distrusting of men, and without hope of ever being in a long-term relationship. He left me with a lot of scars, a lot of emotional baggage, and children who had little respect for me and their dad.

I no longer think that my mom and aunts were totally right. I'd love to turn time back 30 years, but for now I'd even settle for going to the cemetery to get my vagina back if I could.

Sharing my vagina with Paul and Louis and every other married man that I snuck around with behind Paul's back caused a lot of people a lot of pain.

Vagina poem:

Buy the cow or get the milk for free
Tell the man what it's going to be.
Rental agreement or contract for life
Will you be a mistress or will you be a wife?
Think about it and the cost you might pay
There will be consequences for your actions today.
Whatever you do, don't let your vagina be your guide
'Cuz Rose can tell you how her vagina lied.
===================================

REFLECTION AND DISCUSSION

1) What messages do women share with one another that encourage them to have sex and/or be in a relationship with married men?

2) Why do women often believe that they have what it takes to get a married man to leave his wife?

3) What can be done to help women understand potential consequences of being in a relationship with a married man?

4) A growing number of women would rather have sex with a "kept" man, a married man, a bi-sexual man, or someone they can call just for sex. Compare and contrast one of these types of relationships with a more committed relationship like marriage.

CHAPTER 10

SHARING TODAY,

CARING TOMORROW

Sheila was a very attractive 20 year old woman who was in her junior year of college. Until now, Sheila has had a fairly easy life. She grew up in a middle class household and by most accounts experienced very little drama.

Sheila was intelligent, fun to be around, and was considered a charismatic leader. She knew how to mobilize people to get things done. Everyone seemed to like Sheila.

During the winter break from school, life changed for Sheila. Her father was killed in a car accident along with her uncle and two cousins. Sheila was devasted. Her mom insisted that Sheila go back to school because that's what her father and uncle would have wanted. Unfortunately, due to some unknown circumstance, the life insurance policy her parents had on Sheila's dad had lapsed prior to his death. Consequently, Sheila's mom couldn't afford to pay for Sheila to continue at the college she had been attending. After giving it a lot of thought, Sheila agreed that she would return to school, but only on the condition that she is allowed to go back to her same school if she could find a way to cover the tuition, housing, books, and meal plan. Her mom, still grieving her loss and the impact her husband's death was having on her and Sheila, reluctantly agreed to Sheila's request. In her heart, she did not believe Sheila could come up with the money she needed for school in less than 4 weeks.

Sheila sat down with a few close friends to brainstorm ways to generate the close to $14,000 she needed to cover all of the expenses for the spring semester. First on the list was contacting the financial aid office to see what Sheila's options were. Sheila did that and was told that she could have her mom resubmit the financial aid form to show the dramatic change in income. Based on preliminary information, Sheila knew she probably would still need about $5,000 if what the counselor in the financial aid office told her was true. Next on Sheila's list was contacting family, friends, and her church family.

Sunday morning came and Sheila and her mom went to the mid-morning church service. The entire church had been praying for Sheila's family. Since this was the first time after her dad's funeral that Sheila and her mom attended service, the pastor called them to the front of the church to pray for their continued strength and peace. At the end of the prayer, the pastor said he'd like to see them in his office at the end of service.

Sheila and her mom went to the pastor's office as instructed. With a voice that sounded just like James Earl Jones, Pastor Putner got right to the point. Ladies, on behalf of the On My Way to Heaven First Methodist Church of the Baptists, I am pleased to tell you that we have a donation for you in the amount of $7, 545. Sheila and her mom jumped out of their chairs and started screaming and hugging one another. The pastor got up from his chair and gave both of them a hug. He said, "Ladies, much of this money comes from the church. Only part comes from the congregation. We heard that you both could use this money especially for Sheila and school. Since the church treasurer is out of town today, we will have a check for you on this coming Thursday. Although it's a gift, as is customary when we make large donations to members, we ask the recipients to be of service to our congregation in some way." Sheila's mom looked at the pastor and said, "What do you mean, be of service?" The pastor explained that he had several projects that the church could use some assistance with and hoped one or both of them would agree to volunteer.

The three projects on the pastor's list included: 1) taking food to several elderly members on a weekly basis 2) helping to paint classrooms and the recreation center and 3) helping in the office 2-3 days a week for 2-4 hours each day. Sheila and her mom chose to deliver food to the elderly.

Sheila stopped by the pastor's office on Thursday to pick up the check and get the names of the people they were going to be delivering food to. The pastor had not returned from a meeting when Sheila arrived, but his assistant was in. She greeted Sheila and told her that the pastor would be back in about 40 minutes and asked for Sheila to wait if she could. Elated to be picking up the check, Sheila agreed to wait. The assistant struck up a long conversation with Sheila. As it turned out, she was the pastor's niece. The two ladies had a great conversation. Close in age and with similar interests, they agreed to talk more.

The pastor came in a few minutes later and pulled the long awaited check out of his briefcase. He prayed with Sheila as his niece held both of their hands.

Sheila made it a point to go by the church on a weekly basis. She and her pastor would often talk and he continued to pray for her and her mom. One day, while alone with Pastor Putner, he invited Sheila to his home. He told her how much he and his wife cared for her and her mom and hoped that she could get to know his niece a little better. The pastor's niece had been living with them until she could save enough money to get a place of her own.

Sheila went to Pastor Putner's home one Sunday after church. Pastor Putner, his wife, son, niece, and Sheila feasted on a great meal Mrs. Putner prepared. After dinner, they talked, laughed, and played a few games. Before they knew it, it was late. Pastor Putney's wife insisted that Sheila spend the night and assured her that their son or Pastor Putner would take her home in the morning. Sheila agreed then called her mom so she wouldn't worry. The decision to stay and what would occur would haunt Sheila for many years to come.

All Sheila recalls is being awakened around 4 in the morning to something she never expected. Because she was a heavy sleeper, it took a lot to wake her especially if she was tired. So she's not sure what else occurred, but when she woke up, she was in bed with the pastor's niece. Sheila woke up feeling orgasmic and the niece was kissing her on her lips. Blinking her eyes and trying to grasp what was going on, the pastor's niece put her mouth over Sheila's, told her to be quiet or she would tell everyone that Sheila invited her into her room and seduced her. Uncertain what to do and how to deal with what was going on, Sheila lay there and said nothing. The niece kissed her one more time on her lips and said "I love you Sheila" and quietly left the room.

Sheila wanted to go home immediately. She regretted agreeing to spend the night at the pastor's home, and wanted to tell someone, but didn't know if they would believe her.

The next morning, Pastor Putner drove Sheila home. She sat quietly and only heard a few of the many words the pastor said during the 30 minute drive. Sheila felt so ashamed and couldn't imagine who she could tell or what could be done. She decided to say nothing.

Several weeks later, Sheila went back to school. She was happy to be getting back to school and all of the things that occurred over the last few months. Even though the school was three hours away from her home and church, Pastor Putner's niece found a way to visit Sheila at least once or twice a month. Initially, the niece threatened Sheila and said that if she tried to avoid her, she'd tell others what Sheila did to her. Then she started sending Sheila emails thanking her for initiating a love affair with her. Even though Sheila replied to each message saying that it was a lie, the niece opened an email account in Sheila's name and wrote erotic emails as if Sheila was writing them.

Pastor Putner, unaware of what was going on, occasionally drove his niece to Sheila's school to "surprise" her. Sheila's mom, also unaware of the relationship between Sheila and the pastor's niece, thought that Sheila would be pleasantly surprised so she made sure that she knew Sheila would be around when the niece wanted to visit Sheila. Sheila's mom also knew that it wouldn't be a problem for the niece to spend the weekend at the college since Sheila had her own room.

Although Sheila resisted at first, she eventually gave in to the seduction of the pastor's niece. They continued a secret relationship for almost two years until Sheila graduated and accepted a job in Hawaii.

It was ten years later before Sheila returned to her home town for more than a short visit. She was one of the top two candidates for a cabinet position with the governor of her home state. Up to this point, no one knew about the relationship she had with Pastor Putner's niece. Even though Sheila was now married with 2 children, in the back of her mind, she feared someone finding out about the secret life she led for several years. Her fears intensified when she arrived to the interview with the governor and the assistant to his chief of staff was Pastor Putner's niece. The blood felt like it drained from her body when she walked into the room only to be greeted by her former secret lover.

Sheila got the position with the governor. Pastor Putner's niece threatened to reveal their secret unless Sheila went to dinner with her. Instead of allowing her past to remain a secret and give in to the advances of the niece, Sheila told her husband, the governor, and Pastor Putner what happened more than

10 years ago. She was able to move on with her life and the pastor's niece left Sheila alone. Still, whenever Sheila reflects on her life, she says that she would let any woman know that sharing your body with someone you don't want to be with can lead to feelings of shame and fear. Fortunately for Sheila, that same sex relationship didn't stop her from getting appointed to her dream position, but it did cause her a lot of emotional turmoil for many years.

Sheila's message to other women is to count the cost of intimate relationships. Sheila said that women should consider the following: "If I share my body today with a man or woman, will I care tomorrow? Will it cause unhealthy emotions or behavior? If there is a slight possibility of the answer being "yes" to either question, don't share because you probably will care long after the relationship has ended.

REFLECTION AND DISCUSSION

1) We are often encouraged to live in the moment and not be concerned about the future. On the other hand, others say that we must be concerned about what we do today and plan for our future. When it comes to intimacy, what do you believe?

2) Same sex relationships have become a hotly debated topic. Some people think that lesbian relationships are more complicated than heterosexual relationships. What might you share with a female who is contemplating a relationship with another female?

3) In what ways can you support a woman who "found herself" in an intimate relationship with another woman, but doesn't feel good about the relationship? What about a woman who experiences negative emotions while in the relationship or after it's over?

PART II

CHAPTER 11

TIME TO THINK

Part I of this book shared intimate details of the lives of women who wish to reclaim their vagina and erase physical, emotional, financial and social challenges. This section is devoted to examining what women who wish to reclaim their vagina can do. It's clearly understood that there's no way of completely erasing past sexual experiences, but there are ways to move forward in a healthy, productive manner.

If you've responded to the questions at the end of each chapter, you may have important things to share with women about how to move forward. You may have reflected on your past or experiences of family or friends. Now that you've looked back at your experience and the experiences of others, it's time for a metacognitive experience – to think about your thinking about sex and help others make decisions that support women's emotional, physical, and spiritual well-being.

Are you ready? Ok, let's go!

How we behave and think is influenced by many things including our peers, family members or friends, values and beliefs. There's much to be said about the way in which the people around us affect our behavior and attitudes about sex. However, I'd like to focus on two specific influences that I hope you will consider: values and self concept.

In this next section, I'm going to share with you some key strategies to get your values and your behavior in alignment. I will also share strategies for ensuring that your values shape your self concept. As we go through this section, I want you to promise me that you will do two things: 1) think only about yourself and 2) remember that your past is your past. It's important to learn lessons from your past and use them to make better and more informed decisions today and in your future.

Now I need you to promise to do both of these things. Otherwise, if you've had a past that you're not proud of, you might end up experiencing negative emotions and getting stuck. I don't want you to get stuck in negative emotions and thoughts. The idea behind this section is to help you think about some of the things that influence how you decide whether to engage in sexual acts and to arm yourself with tools necessary to make decisions that don't lead to your wanting your vagina back! Does that make sense? Alright, let's get started.

After talking to countless women who wish they could get their vagina back, I started wondering why we keep sharing our bodies with men that we end up wishing we hadn't. So I began to listen to the conversations of women. I wanted to hear what seemed to drive them to have sex with multiple partners, to engage in risky sexual behavior, and to ultimately end up regretting many of their experiences. I also thought about my experiences and did a lot of soul searching. After listening and observing others and thinking about my life, I began to see a pattern. Regardless of whether a woman was poor and struggling to make ends meet or wealthy and living an extravagant life, I realized that in many cases, women know exactly what they're getting into. It's not that they are always getting drunk or being raped or getting caught up in the moment. No, in many cases, women are making conscious decisions to engage in sex even when they aren't all that interested in the man. Do you know what many single women have said are primary reasons they have sex? They wanted to AND it was a way of connecting with a man. There's nothing deep about that is there?

Some women think about the consequences of their behavior after they've engaged in sex. On the other hand other women consider the possible consequences prior to engaging in sex, but still choose to take the risk. Which one are you?

My daughter recently told me I was a "consequentialist." As far back as she can remember, I would say to her and my son that they not only needed to choose in life, but to be ready to live with the consequences of their choices. While I think that that can be an effective approach, I've also learned that thinking about the consequences is not enough. Why? Because I might not know about all of the consequences. I might think that I'm making a wise decision, but it can only be wise to the degree of knowledge and information I have. Here's an example:

> Charlene meets Greg. They go out for almost a year without engaging in any sexual activity. Greg and Charlene spend a lot of time learning about one another and although they both want to wait to be married to have sex, the sexual tension between them is getting stronger.

> Charlene has done her homework. She knows that Greg has not been with a lot of women and has shared with her that he has been abstinent for the last 2 years. During his last doctor's visit, Greg told Charlene that he had been tested for HIV and other STDs, and according to the lab results, had no STDs.

One night, Charlene, who, by the way is a virgin, decides that it will be ok if she had sex with Greg. Since they're going to get married, she doesn't feel that having premarital sex will make that much of a difference. After dinner, they go to her apartment and have sexual intercourse. Charlene wakes up the next morning feeling extreme guilt. She feels like she just made the worst mistake in her life, but there's nothing she can do. Charlene tries to comfort herself using self-talk. "I'm going to be married to Greg soon. What we did is ok."

Several weeks before Greg and Charlene's wedding, Charlene surprises Greg one evening. He's working late so Charlene decides to go to Greg's apartment, fix him dinner, and make it a special night for the two of them.

Charlene is the one who gets surprised when she goes into the apartment using her key and finds Greg in bed with another man. Greg eventually confesses that he has been living on the down low for several years. He apologizes profusely, but Charlene is devastated. She cancels the wedding. Months later, Charlene tested positive for HIV. Greg had been having unprotected sex with men.

With slight variations in the story, what happened to Charlene is what has happened to a number of women. Charlene never intended to contract HIV. She believed what Greg told her and thought that since she would be marrying him, having sex with Greg prior to marriage would be ok. The reality is, unless Greg was honest and told Charlene about his lifestyle or unless Greg was tested for HIV and showed Charlene his results (not fake results), she might not have found out about Greg's HIV status until after the wedding.

The bottom line is that Charlene had information, knowledge, and considered her options, but made a decision that changed her life. This change was something she would have to live with forever.

This is a story where Charlene wanted to have sex with Greg and rationalized her decision to go for it.

Here are a few questions to consider when faced with a decision to have sex or not:

1) Is having sex at this time consistent with my values?

2) Why do I want to have sex? Why with this person?

3) What are the potential known consequences and unintended consequences if I engage in sex at this time?

4) How will I feel if the relationship with this man ends or if I contract an STD?

Let's explore each of these questions in a little more detail.

Question #1: IS HAVING SEX AT THIS TIME CONSISTENT WITH MY VALUES?

What are your core values? What are the beliefs that drive you on a daily basis? This is really important for you to think about. Don't gloss over this question, but give it serious thought. You should be able to identify your top 5 values. Use the space in Appendix A and jot down your top 5 values. There's space for 10 in case you think of more than 5.

If you aren't sure what your top 5 values are or if your values don't serve as a guide for your behavior, that may be why you have at least one situation where you'd like to go and get your vagina back.

To assist you with this, let me give you a definition of "values": Values are the "beliefs of a person….in which they have an emotional investment" (Wordreference.com). Values are beliefs that guide how a person thinks, act, or speak in many cases. Examples of values include respect, love, integrity, honesty, and friendship.

A few words people use that communicate values include "should, should not, must, and ought to." An example of a statement that speaks someone's values might be: "You should leave that man. He's no good for you." The statement reflects the communicator's values which may not be consistent with the values of the person the message was communicated to. What makes a woman think someone should leave another person? It's her values. Although in some cases, experiences (positive and negative) will also influence our responses and behavior, frequently, the messages that we speak reflect our personal values.

If your behavior is inconsistent with your personal values, it might cause you to experience internal turmoil. It might also result in your dealing with situations that you wish you didn't have to deal with.

If the character and/or actions of individuals you're in relationships with don't line up with your values, you can also expect to experience frustration, anxiety, or shame. For instance, if you identify honesty as one of your values, but keep allowing your inner circle to consist of people who are prevaricators, your values and your behavior are incongruent. If you truly value honesty, you are likely to be uncomfortable having people around you who intentionally and regularly lie. As another example, if you believe in abstaining from sex until you're married, but you have sex without being married, you might experience shame, guilt, resentment, and a variety of emotional issues.

The key here is when it comes to your sexual behavior, it is important for you to be clear about your values and allow your values to guide your actions, who you enter into a relationship with, and your communication. If you do this, you will experience a life where you have fewer or no doors that you want to knock on and say "Can I have my vagina back?"

Question #2: WHY DO I WANT TO HAVE SEX? WHY WITH THIS PERSON?

The answer to this may vary well be "it depends." But let me submit to you that it's a fundamental question worth exploring. To understand why you want to have sex with a person (excluding a marital partner) will help you explore some of your inner most feelings and thoughts. For instance, there are some women who say that they have sex to relieve stress. Others say that it's something they enjoy doing. Those reasons may be true, but let's see if we can get behind those "on the surface" reasons.

We have hormones that influence our feelings, appearance, and attitudes. For instance, as a result of hormones, some women develop more or less body hair (including those dreaded chin and mustache hairs that we spend too much time picking). In some cases, women experience symptoms of PMS. Maybe that's not you, but there were times when I thought my head was about to turn around on my body. Something would happen a few days prior to my period that would cause me to feel emotional, irritable, happy, sad, and many other emotions around the same time. At times, I felt like I was going crazy. I think the people closest to me may have thought the same thing.

Because of the impact our hormones have on the body, companies have developed a variety of products to combat symptoms of PMS and to quickly remove or permanently destroy unwanted hair. We will pop a pill, stay in bed, or go to an esthetician or other specialist to remove facial and other hair. We'll do almost anything to control the effects or symptoms of our raging hormones.

What do we do when it comes to our feelings and desire for sex? Many women know the possible consequences of having sex, but still engage in sexual acts only to try and fix things later or when it's too late. Maybe it's like what we do for the facial hair and emotions – we react instead of being proactive. Why do we do that? Why do we wait until after contracting an STD to decide to insist that a man use a condom during intercourse?

A friend, who is a nurse, once told me that women come to her all week long to get medication for one venereal disease or another. Unfortunately, she says that many of those same women come back month after month for the same venereal disease. Not only is repeatedly contracting venereal diseases or infections unhealthy for a female's body, it is unwise to place yourself at risk of contracting something that is not curable. Is sex so good that it's worth dying for? If your answer is yes, then what? Please don't say, "Well at least I'll die having enjoyed sex." Whatever your answer, you're communicating your values and self worth.

In addition to why we have sex, there's the issue of why we have sex with the men we choose to sleep with. Have you ever thought about this? Some research has been done to explore the effects of sexual behavior. It has been said that when you allow a man to enter your body, that a connection is established that may not easily be broken. For some women, the connection is psychological and lasts for many years. Have you ever wondered why months and years after a relationship is over you keep thinking about a man you slept with even though he was abusive, manipulative, and not worth your time? Some would say that's because there's a "soul tie" between you and that man. So if you're trying to figure out why you're depressed, mad, or acting like the M&M candy on the commercial that doesn't want the pretzel inside of it, it just might be because your connection to a past lover did not end when the sex ended. If you've slept with a number of men, you might want to consider how those relationships have affected you emotionally in the past or how they're still affecting you.

Answering the questions "Why do I have sex and why with the partner(s) I have chosen" are critical to making healthy lifestyle decisions. Saying "because I choose to or want to" is not good enough. It may be your first response, but doesn't get to your inner most feelings and thoughts.

If you're going to choose to do something like having sex, I'm hoping you will be comfortable with your choice and fully aware of how it could impact your life. There are already too many women regretting past sexual experiences. Whether you are one of them or not, I hope you will try and understand the importance of being thoughtful and intentional in your decision making. A decision to have sex is not one to be taken lightly.

I do recognize that when you're in the heat of a passionate moment, you are not as likely to run through the series of questions that I asked. What I'm hoping is that if you're clear about your values and allow your values to inform your decision making, then there is a possibility that in a moment of passion, your action will line up with your values. I'm hoping that you will find your voice and say no. This my friend will lead to fewer regrets and fewer negative outcomes.

Questions #3: What are the potential consequences and unintended consequences if I engage in sex at this time?

For every action, there is a possible consequence and an unintended consequence that can be positive or negative. Sometimes you can clearly see the possible consequences, but you also want to be concerned about the unintended consequences – the ones you might not be aware of at the time you decide to have sex.

It's like the story of the woman who contracted HIV from a man she thought she was marrying. In a relationship where there is love, trust and mutual respect, I believe that a couple should consider disclosing anything that can affect their relationship or one another. There shouldn't be any surprises like in the case of one woman who found out after she was married, that her husband had two children (one was born right after they started dating, the other right before they got married) and debt with a former wife that he was still responsible for.

A person shouldn't mind getting tested for HIV and other sexually transmitted diseases. Test results can help both partners be informed and choose how to proceed in the relationship if the test results are negative or positive. In the absence of lab results, partners possibly enter relationships without the benefit of knowing important information about one another.

The marriage counseling at the church I attend included a requirement that you get tested for STDs, review each other's credit report, and pull child support documents if either partner was a non-custodial parent. My husband to be and I had no problem fulfilling this requirement. The results of our tests and the credit reports led to a healthy discussion. We entered our marriage with no surprises unlike the woman previously described. As you can imagine, she was hurt, angry, and began to distrust anything her husband said to her. This couple's marriage ended after only two years.

Another example of an unintended consequence is being sued by the wife of a man you slept with. Watch out for those fine, smooth talking, wearing the right cologne men who make you want to melt in their arms and give them your panties. Some are married and may not disclose their marital status until after you have strong feelings for them. Others will disclose the truth about their marital status and say they're separated or planning to leave the wife. Please keep in mind that a married man may not be telling you the truth when he says he's in the process of separating from his wife. Being in an intimate relationship with such a man can be costly.

In some states, legislation has been passed which allows a wife to sue her husband's "mistress" for "alienation of affection" and violation of the marriage contract. One woman was awarded $9 million dollars for her husband's infidelity. Although the wife may not ever collect the $9 million dollars from the mistress, the outcome of the case sent a powerful message to women who choose to be in a relationship with a married man.

There are too many known and unknown consequences of engaging in sex with someone. Think it through carefully and decide whether having sex lines up with your values as well as what having sex will do to the value of your vagina.

Here's another way to think of it: If you were in possession of a piece of art that several auctioneers confirmed was unique and worth at least millions of dollars, what would you do to preserve its value? Well my friend, I believe you're a unique woman with a value that far exceeds millions of dollars. Now the question becomes, what will you do to preserve your body so that it doesn't lose its value?

Question #4: HOW WILL I POSSIBLY FEEL ABOUT HAVING SEX WITH THIS MAN IF THE RELATIONSHIP ENDS SOONER THAN I THINK OR IF I CONTRACT AN STD?

When deciding whether to have sex or not, women need to think about MMI: ME, MYSELF, AND I.

Engaging in sex is a personal act, but it can have implications long after the day or night you had sex. Let's look at some of the possibilities:

> You may have to spend time going to the doctors for yeast or bacterial infections, STDs, precancerous or cancerous cells, unexplained pain in the vagina, lesions, and swelling or vaginal tears. Then there's the cost for time missed from work or other activities, the cost for out of pocket expenses like co-pays if you have insurance and prescriptions and over the counter medication. Your time is precious and can be better spent on things that are more desirable, pleasurable, and productive.

- You might experience emotional highs
and lows. Tell me something. After
you've engaged in sex with someone
you wished you hadn't, how has that
affected you? Have you been moody,
irritable, and upset? What about those
of you who don't want to be bothered
and avoid people, or get depressed, and
call friends crying or complaining for
more time than they'd like to spend on
the subject?, Then there are the times
when you avoid people or cause them to
be distant because of your nasty or
negative behavior? This may not be a
big deal to you, but it should be. There
are family, friends, and others who care
about your emotional and physical well-
being. When you make bad choices
when it comes to your sexual behavior,
it can affect you and others who
sometimes wish they could shake some
sense in you.

=====================================

REFLECTION AND DISCUSSION

There's so much that could be said about each of the 4 questions that I just discussed. However, I want to give you an opportunity to talk with others about these questions. Here's what I'd like for you to do:

Call another woman or pull together a small group and discuss the four questions. If you're not comfortable talking about your experiences or if you don't have experiences that you regret, have a conversation with someone to discuss other women you care about. Identify someone to be the recorder. I'd like for you to leave the discussion with several things:

1) Responses to why women really choose to have sex, not just what they say.

2) Ideas about what led to good decisionmaking. Specifically, what stopped a woman from having sex when she had the desire to have sex, but really didn't want to at that time?

3) Information on ways women can learn to value themselves enough to make healthy, wise choices when it comes to their sexual behavior.

4) Resources to help women who are experiencing negative emotional, physical, or financial issues as a result of a sexual relationship.

After you've talked about each of the four questions previously identified and have covered the four assignments above, have the recorder summarize the discussion. Add anything you believe is important. Make copies of the summary or email it to one another and use it as a resource for future discussions and for women needing help.

CHAPTER 12

MOVING FORWARD

To some, the body is sacred, a temple. It is a living organism that is comprised of interdependent parts. When one part of the body is damaged or destroyed, it affects other parts of the body.

It's interesting that we place high value on parts that seem most important to us while ignoring other parts of the body or treating them as if they're a recyclable or replaceable commodity. The head, for instance, is something we protect as much as possible. We don't allow others to bang us in the head on a regular basis nor do we hit our head up against a wall with the intention of damaging it – at least not if we're sane.

Many women take really good care of their hands, feet, and hair with regular manicures,

111

pedicures, and hair grooming. Many of us get facials, massages, and waxing services on a regular basis.

What parts of your body do you focus a lot of attention on? Why?

Once again, I ask the question, "How much value do you place on your vagina?

If you could place a price tag on your vagina, would it be a thrift store price, free, or a price that you'd see in the most expensive store you can think of?

As women, if we're going to have fewer regrets in life, we should make values-driven decisions. Some might ask what's wrong with carefree, risky, live for the moment kind of living that involves casual sex, regular sex, or "oops, I didn't mean to end up in bed with you" sex? Instead of a values-driven response, I'll simply suggest that you consider the outcomes for each of the women described in the stories in this book and others. Once gain, I'd like for you to consider the following possible outcomes of sex that leads to regrets:

112

- Unwanted pregnancy

- Curable & incurable STDs (including HPV, HIV/AIDS)

- Depression and other negative psychological outcomes

- Damaged or irritated vaginal lining

- Unexpected doctor's visits & expenses

- Shame, anger, resentment, bitterness

- Feelings of distrust

- Difficulty having healthy sexual relations

- Missed time from work or school

- Separation from family and/or friends

- What else can you think of?

CHAPTER 13

WHERE DO YOU GO FROM HERE?

Take a deep breath and exhale. If you did that and you're reading this book, that means you are alive and have another opportunity to make good choices for your life. Don't be so hard on yourself if you've shared your body with one or more people. Start with this moment and live to minimize your regrets. It's up to you and I believe you can make today and all of your tomorrows better than your past. So why not start right now?

To help you be reflective, I encourage you to purchase a journal or use one that you already have. A journal can be used to further explore your thinking and actions when it comes to sex.

Journaling is a useful tool for expressing your innermost thoughts and feelings. It's also a nice way of writing things that you wouldn't say or share with others. Remember it is a

114

great tool for expressing yourself and useful when you don't have anyone you feel comfortable talking with. I encourage you to write from your heart without fear or reservation. It's your journal, your feelings, and your life.

You can use your journal as a message to your daughter(s), your niece(s), little sister(s) or anyone else you'd like to share important messages with.

Journal for the next 90 days. Take about 5-10 minutes each day to write something in your journal. Be sure to record the date of each entry. Choose a time of day to write and stick with that time as much as you can. You don't have to write about only things related to sex. The idea is to use the journal as a means to better understand your thoughts, feelings, and decision-making related to sex. You may discover patterns of behavior or see a relationship between your actions or way of thinking and that of your mother, grandmother or other women in your life. What I expect is that after 90 days, you will discover something

115

about yourself that is meaningful, important, and insightful.

Journaling can be fun, therapeutic, and useful on your life's journey. I have used journals for many years. Months or years later when I go back and read some of my entries, I frequently laugh at myself or simply shake my head in disbelief at some of my thoughts and behaviors. Thank God for time and grace!

The questions in this book can evoke myriad emotions. Therefore, it is important that you talk about your feelings with someone you feel you can trust. The questions were not intended for you to examine alone. That's why the section at the end of each chapter is called "Reflection and Discussion."

I expect that discussions will continue long after you have closed this book and placed it on a bookshelf or shared it with another woman.

A person you trust in a safe environment can offer wise counsel, help you process your feelings, and possibly shift your perspective and behavior if necessary. As previously mentioned, consider consulting a trained professional or spiritual advisor if you have difficulty dealing with or managing negative emotions after reading this book. You don't have to feel bad about past sexual experiences or consequences you are living with. Regardless of what you've done, you deserve to move beyond your past and live a purposeful, joyful life while making the best decisions each day of your life.

I have talked with and listened to too many women who wanted to erase some of their sexual experiences. They would give anything to change the past. In many cases, women have learned important lessons from those experiences. Some might say that "experience is the best teacher." When it comes to sex, I would disagree. In this case, I would say let the experiences of others be your best teacher.

By reading the stories in Part I of this book, I hope you have been stirred to make wise choices and to dialogue with women to help them do the same.

If you are a woman who has no desire or reason to pick up a container, knock on some doors to ask for your vagina back, then good for you. I hope that you will share with other girls and women how you have come to have few regrets related to your sexual behavior. If you're a pretender who wears a mask and acts like everything is fine when it's really not, please don't encourage others to be pretenders. Denying your feelings or simply saying that you live for the moment is not the best way to make decisions when it comes to deciding whether to engage in sex.

Sex can be a wonderful, satisfying experience. It can be something you look forward to and an experience that brings you closer to your partner. Let me be clear - sex may not lead to any negative outcomes for you as previously discussed. You have some control over that if you are proactive and are values driven.

Today, there are efforts all over the world to decrease teen pregnancy, sexual abuse, and the number of women contracting STDs, especially HIV/AIDS. Faith-based organizations including a number of churches and youth organizations have purity ceremonies during which females take a vow of abstinence and receive a ring as a symbol of their commitment to God and self. The idea is to encourage positive sexual behavior and help women live a happier, healthier life.

My friend, I would not have written this book if I didn't care about you. I believe that I "am my sister's keeper." I am on a mission and I need your help. So do me a favor, care enough for another female to spread this message. Share with at least one woman the affirmation at the end of the book (Appendix B).Tell her your story or one of the ones in this book. Tell her that even though you can't live her life, you have some things to share that might lead to a healthy, joyous future. Tell your sisters, your daughters, your nieces, their friends, and any other female that can be helped. That's my final assignment for you.

My hope is that this book starts a movement – one that begins with you. I hope that the stories and questions contained throughout this book have challenged you to examine your sexual behavior and thinking about sex. I hope that it has caused you to place more value on your body than you do your jewelry, nails, hair, or other personal possessions. I hope that it has reminded you that it's ok to say "no" when someone else wants you to say "yes." I hope that it reminds you that you don't have to share your vagina even when your vagina would like you to. I hope that this book has encouraged you to talk with another female about sex and the value of her vagina. I hope that something in this book will save a life, save the quality of someone's life, and finally, keep someone from proclaiming as too many of us have, "I want my vagina back."

APPENDIX A

PERSONAL VALUES

List of my top 5-10 values:

Example: love, integrity, friendship, family

1.

2.

3.

4.

5.

6.

7.

8.

9.

10.

APPENDIX B

VALUING MY VAGINA
AFFIRMATION

I CHOOSE TO VALUE MY VAGINA
MORE THAN THE THINGS I BUY OR
BORROW
I CHOOSE TO TREAT IT WITH CARE
AND PROTECT IT TODAY AND
TOMORROW

I DECIDE WHEN ACCESS IS GRANTED
AND WILL PRESERVE MY VAGINA'S
UTILITY
I WON'T SELL IT OR AUCTION IT TO THE
HIGHEST BIDDER
NO MATTER HOW I FEEL ABOUT ONE'S
CAPABILITY

I CHOOSE TO TEACH ANOTHER FEMALE
HOW TO VALUE HER VAGINA AND HAVE
SELF WORTH
I WILL TELL HER THAT CHOICES HAVE
CONSEQUENCES
AND TO MAKE THE MOST OF LIFE ON
THIS EARTH

I CHOOSE TO FORGIVE MYSELF AND
OTHERS
FOR WHAT I DID AND DID NOT CHOOSE
TO HAPPEN TO ME
I WON'T BE DEFINED BY MY CHOICES OR
CIRCUMSTANCES
I WILL PLAY A PART IN DIRECTING MY
DESTINY

I CHOOSE TO VALUE MY VAGINA
AND LOVE MY BODY, MIND AND SOUL
MY CHOOSING TO VALUE MY VAGINA
IS PART OF MY CHOOSING TO LIVE
HEALTHY, FREE, AND WHOLE

"DR LOVE" (2010)

CONTACTING DR. PAM LOVE

To share your testimonial about "*I Want My Vagina Back*" or to invite Dr. Love to speak:

Email: lifedestination357@yahoo.com

Mail: PM Love Enterprises, Inc.
            P.O. Box 47133
            Baltimore, Md. 21244

For additional information about how you can order additional products and services by Dr. Love and to see what else she is doing, visit www.drpamlove.com